The *Journey*

"The truth is that our finest moments are most likely to occur when we are feeling deeply uncomfortable, unhappy, or unfulfilled.

For it is only in such moments, propelled by our discomfort, that we are likely to step out of our ruts and start searching for different ways or truer answers."

~ *M. Scott Peck* ~

The *Journey*

"How <u>not</u> to get kicked out of Earth University (EU)"

Lucy Shaw

Florida

The *Journey*

Copyright © 2016 Lucy Shaw

All rights reserved.

XMS Publishing

1391 NW St. Lucie West Blvd, Suite 247

Port St. Lucie, FL 34986

This publication is designed to provide accurate and authoritative information regarding the subject matter covered. It is sold with the understanding that the publisher is not engaged in rendering legal, accounting, medical, or other professional services.

The information and opinions presented in this book are intended for educational purposes only. Any income claims or results discussed in this book are not typical, and they are for example only.

ISBN-13: 978-0692785737

ISBN-10: 0692785736

Published in the United States of America

Dedication

This book is for all of the prayers answered; miracles wrought; and my many failed, repeated, and passed tests here at Earth University.

It is also for all of the amazing people past, present, and future who honor me with the privilege of being a tutor and coach on their *JOURNEY* and matriculation through Earth University.

With much love,

Lucy

What Others Say About Working with Lucy

Hi Lucy,

Below is a personal statement about how I felt before and what I am feeling after our coaching sessions. Now, I know that we did indeed take a *Journey*! I do appreciate you and all you did for me.

When I engaged Lucy, I didn't know what to expect. I knew something was "off kilter" in my personal and professional environment; not bad, just not entirely whole. I reached out to her on a reference from a trusted partner. What I learned after an eight-week Life Coaching commitment was that the majority of my issues were not about the external factors, as I first thought (although I had allowed them to drain my energy!).

I am very good at what I do for a living. But, for forty-plus years, struggling and climbing to get ahead in this world, I neglected to learn necessary survival skills to take care of my inside self. Lucy taught me valuable tools and techniques to recognize, harness, and pull myself back to center (or the Nexus as she calls it). Lucy instructed me on how to look at things through a different lens and taught me many new techniques for working through issues to reach a healthier, more complete perspective.

Additionally, Lucy made herself available through an array of avenues so I could reach her when I needed assistance with a new technique. Although I may not have mastered every technique, I can tell you with confidence that I feel more whole. Lucy's knowledge, experience, teaching approach, and patience were truly a blessing for me.

Oh, and I am in round two with an application for a new job opportunity! It is like you said, the more you give, the more you receive be it time, money, etc. I am beginning to see that. Those words made a big impact.

Thanks for being you,
Lori

Table of Contents

INTRODUCTION

The Testimonial at the beginning of this book is rather typical of the feedback I get from those who trust me to travel with them briefly. I want to do for people what I had no one to do for me during my many periods of being stuck on my way to greater and greater experiences of happiness and success. Most successful people will tell you that the public and private side of success can be as rewarding as winning the lottery, but the movement to the next big level of growth often takes periods of deep uncertainty, discomfort, and painful discipline. My most profound and memorable "crash and burn" left me lying on my sofa, looking out at the river every day, trying to figure out where I went wrong and where I wanted to go if I ever got better!

I was President and CEO of an academic medical center and safety net hospital. My professional career began as a bedside nurse and teacher, then a manager, an administrator, a vice president, a chief operating officer,

1

and finally the top executive. I had been mentored by some of the very best. But leadership and the appropriately long *Journey* to it can be tough if you don't accept that the humility required for learning how to lead is quite different from the humility that helps us to serve others.

While there are great writings available about what is called *Servant Leadership*, my sense is that there is a path upon which we learn the art and mechanics of Leadership and yet another where we learn the art and mechanics of taking care of ourselves while we are serving. At some point in our individual and unique process of development or evolution, the two merge and we learn to balance our relationships with God, Self, Others, and a Purpose that serves all. And as if that is not enough, we have a Self to handle that, all by "itself," makes emotional, intellectual, spiritual, and physical demands. This is the biggest Leadership assignment of all being CEO of your life!

The good news is that these parts of us work in harmony even when we don't feel like that's the case. If you have ever *felt* too tired to think, too hungry to be nice, too emotional to pray, or too stupid to fix any of it, then you know what I mean. Success at Leading and Serving is not for the faint of heart! And any form of success requires both. In this book, I will share some of my secrets and strategies for leading and serving in the life of my most important client ME. Then I will share some of the steps I take with clients when I am engaged in sharing their *Journey*. I am usually invited to join another's *Journey* when they get stuck and find themselves feeling uncomfortable, unhappy, or unfulfilled.

> **For me, living a life of abundant joy, purpose, and loving kindness is the whole point of matriculating on this planet through what I like to call Earth University.**

For me, living a life of abundant joy, purpose, and loving kindness is the whole point of matriculating on this planet through what I like to call *Earth University*. Yet, the promise of abundant living is not without the constant demand for studying, taking tests, failing, passing, and when all is right, moving on to the next class.

Before you begin reading, be warned! I will talk about knowing and having something bigger than yourself to rely upon. I call this God. You may have another name for it. Shucks, I may even talk about prayer (which, by the way, we all do, whether we call it that or not!). The foreplay to happiness and success can be, and often is, a series of humbling experiences, and the sooner we understand that, the happier and more successful we will become.

IN PURSUIT OF THE RIGHT TOOLS

"For I know the plans I have for you," declares the LORD, "plans to prosper you and not to harm you, plans to give you hope and a future." Jeremiah 29:11 KJV

"To the man who only has a hammer, everything he encounters begins to look like a nail." Abraham Maslow

Life Coach. Really? Author. Really? Not having a "real" job for over 20 years. Self-employed. Really? Widowed. Really? National teacher, speaker, facilitator. Really?

I had ignored all of the physical signs of stress for years, as I became more and more successful. I ignored the mental, emotional, and physical clues that all was not well. In fact, I lulled myself to sleep believing that my prayer life was tight and that I had nothing to worry about. I was a spiritual snob. Eventually, though, I also felt spiritually bereft, lost, and like a big fat hypocrite. While I occupied myself by trying to save everyone in my little corner of the world, in my hospital, and in my community, I was gradually being consumed by physical fatigue, emotional and mental strain, and the isolation of being a self-appointed "she-ro." Even my mind hurt. I couldn't think. I had lost the capacity to really, really be coherent in my thinking. That's how sick I was. That's how empty I was because I was into giving, never receiving. Having fallen into the success trap of needing to have all the answers, I didn't have anybody to confide in because that might make me appear vulnerable.

My husband and I had only been married a short while, and his first wife had sickened suddenly and quickly passed away of cancer. So he was no help to me. He saw his new bride whom he loved dearly, suddenly getting sick, barely able to function and looking like she too was dying. In hindsight, it wasn't sudden, as he, like me, refused to acknowledge my progressive illness and relentless fatigue. When people would call to say, "How is Lucy doing?" he'd say, "Oh she's doing great!" He went straight to denial, so I didn't have any support at home either!

Frankly, I just know in my heart that there are so many successful people who go into a dark night of the soul and don't have anybody to help bring them through. Like Lori, it may just feel like something is "off kilter." Sometimes they don't even know they are entering a dark night of the soul.

> **I began Coaching because my own experience brought me to the need to learn how to re-create myself physically, mentally, emotionally, and spiritually again and again. I learned that there is no part of me that can be left alone or allowed to fragment.**

I began Coaching because my experience brought me to the need to learn how to re-create myself physically, mentally, emotionally, and spiritually again and again. I discovered that there is no part of me that can be left alone or allowed to fragment. I, like you, am a whole person, and I am 100% responsible for what shows up in my life. Most of all, this life we all have is totally analogous to a *Journey*. No matter how well-planned we think we've made our path, there is a much bigger, smarter, more powerful Master Planner who orchestrates rest stops, detours, exit signs, off ramps, and all sorts of curious stuff to keep us on our toes, humble, and growing. My passion is for this wonder-filled *Journey* and our necessary capacity to grasp the wonder without being so painfully attached to the destination. When I get a letter like the one I got from Lori, it just tells me once again, "Yes, Lucy, you're doing some really worthwhile work with some really cool people!"

FOOD FOR THE *JOURNEY*

Throughout this book, there will be questions and comments called "Food for the *Journey.*" These are, in part, the kinds of challenges I use with my clients (business, personal, and professional) to help them assess and find answers for the feelings, beliefs, and behaviors that cause them to get stuck! The questions will be probing and should be answered in a quiet, safe space. If they make you nervous or anxious, I strongly suggest that you go to Amazon and download my book, **Be Not Anxious**, and learn Emotional Freedom Technique (EFT). You may also go to my website, www.lifeworkswithlucy.com, and download the instructions. This is one of the techniques I use in my Coaching practice to help clients identify and work through beliefs, emotions, and behaviors that get and keep them stuck.

MY *JOURNEY*:
CRYSTAL STAIRS AND EXIT SIGNS

So, boy, don't you turn back.
Don't you set down on the steps.
'Cause you finds it's kinder hard.
Don't you fall now.
For I'se still goin', honey,
I'se still climbin',
And life for me ain't been no crystal stair.

Langston Hughes, *Mother to Son*

PASSION AND DISCIPLINE

I think what qualifies me more than anything to be a really, really good coach and intuitive facilitator (and that's not brag, but the result of passion and discipline) is that I have, by necessity, developed a deep sense of self-compassion. Successful folk are their own worst (or best) critics. It would be really difficult for somebody to come to me and talk to me or share anything with me that I have not had an opportunity to feel, do, or witness. Of course, I haven't murdered anybody, but I tell you what, I know that in my lifetime, I have killed some relationships, or killed the "spirit" of others in relationships, and so, in that sense, yeah, maybe I've committed a much ignored form of murder. The point is, I have no room to judge others. Maybe I can give you some painful insight, though!

FOOD FOR THE *JOURNEY*

1. What are you really passionate about? Is it something you do well but don't get to do enough of? Why not?

2. What does discipline look and feel like to you? One of the most chronicled and widely read *Journeys* is the one taken by the twelve followers of Jesus the Christ. These guys were called *disciples*. Wonder why? Over and over, they were learning the power of discipline. Their Coach was awesome! He demanded discipline. He was a stickler for three things that I use as a Coach:

    a. Know and love your God and know why.

    b. Know and love yourself and know why.

    c. Know and love those you choose to help or serve and know why.

"HOW DO I GET RID OF OLIVE OYL, DAUGHTER OF COLE OYL AND NANA OYL?"

I was raised in a family of really, really smart people. My Mom gave birth to seven children, and my dad was 40 years older than my mom. My baby sister is 10 years younger than me, born when my Mom was 40 and my Dad 80. My dad had a recipe for how that works and told my mom, who told my brothers. That is a different story, a different book.

I never thought I was good enough, pretty enough, smart enough, tall enough, dark enough, and certainly not curvy enough.

My parents were extremely smart and resourceful. They were successful black entrepreneurs in a time when that was not a common string of words, possibly even an oxymoron. My father was not an easy man to live with and caused my mom a lot of heartache. In her zeal to help me learn to be self-sufficient, strong, and never dependent on a man, I picked up a profound challenge to be worthy and to please. I never thought I was good enough, pretty enough, smart enough, tall enough, dark enough, and certainly not curvy enough.

My nickname was "Olive Oyl" until I was 16. (If you don't know who Olive Oyl is you are either too young to be reading this book or you need to use your Google skills.) I could easily find a thousand things wrong with myself. I don't think I even learned to appreciate myself physically until I was almost 40 years old. That's how long my *Journey* into self-compassion lasted!

FOOD FOR THE *JOURNEY*

1. Do you deserve to be happy? Really? Pay attention to the little, small voice that has a "Yes, but…"
2. Could you do what you do better, even when others tell you what a great job you just did? Do you always ask questions like:
   a. Was I good enough?
   b. Did I do enough homework or research?
   c. Did I look good enough? Why didn't I wear that other dress or suit?
   d. If only I was….?
3. From where did you get that habitual questioning and self-doubt?
4. When you do things that come easily to you and people ooh and ahh over it, do you sometimes feel like a hypocrite?

"I was lookin' for love in all the wrong places." (*Vocals by Johnny Lee)*

And as if He was lost, I started searching for God in my 20's, going through religious denominations and movements like an excited, hungry child in a candy store. I picked up bits and pieces of spirituality, which encouraged the need to have a personal and individual relationship with God and a little bit of religious bigotry that allowed others to dictate how

12

that relationship should look. I spent years finding a right measure of sustainable faith and belief in the object of my Search.

In the midst of all of that self-criticism and self-judgment, I was very successful in any work I chose to do. In spite of what I thought about myself, it turned out that I was smart, attractive, and a disciplined and eager learner. I also wanted to please and to do the right thing. More than anything, my mother had insisted that my first plan should always be to leave a place, or the people in it, better off than I found it and them. That was my standard for self-measurement, even if it meant not attending to my needs.

I married several times, and those marriages failed. My fourth marriage (yep, I said 4th) was the charm. Sometimes you just have to kiss a lot of frogs to find your prince. And sometimes, all along, *you* are the frog!

It was not until I woke up one day, right after my third divorce, and had a good conversation with God and said, "You know what God? I've figured this out. I get married for all the wrong reasons. I get married thinking that someone else is responsible for my happiness and end up seriously p----- off when they don't succeed! So here's the deal, God. I'm not doing it anymore. If *YOU* don't send somebody else into my life, I just won't have anybody for the rest of my life. I'm finished with the looking. I'm not looking anymore because I clearly don't do this well." That was the best thing that ever happened to me, and I stayed single that time, longer than I had ever been single in my young adult life. I also began to learn some wonderful things about myself along the way.

FOOD FOR THE *JOURNEY*

1. Do you have an intentional method for testing the "rightness" of what you do? Here are a few clues:
   a. You have learned to respect and respond to your "gut" reactions to situations, circumstances, and hunches.
   b. You make sure that there is some good in it for someone other than yourself.
   c. You don't compromise your values or seek expediency. When we are expedient, we do what's convenient. People have been killed for the sake of expediency Jesus, Dr. Martin Luther King, and President Kennedy to name a few.
   d. Will you need to "take a knee" and ask and receive help from a higher power to reach your goal?
   e. Can you discipline yourself not to get caught up in pleasing others for the sake of praise, approval, and getting ahead?
   f. Do you understand the principle of "harmless as a dove, wise as a serpent"?
2. Are you taking 100% responsibility for what shows up in your life? Responsibility is not the same as blame or guilt. Blame means it is someone else's fault. Guilt means you think it's your fault. Responsibility means you intentionally exercise your

power to confidently imagine and pursue a bigger, better, more enriching outcome in every moment!

"Trust in the Lord with all your heart and lean not on your own understanding; in all your ways submit to him, and he will make your paths straight." **Proverbs 3:5, 6 NKJV**

The trick with surrender, however, is that God's being in charge does not free us of personal responsibility, choosing, or informed effort.

A significant discovery for me during that time was how to trust in God. You can call it a higher power or however you want to express it. I learned how to trust that God could very well, with no help from me, be in charge of my life. I surrendered, and that's when I learned first-hand about the whole notion of surrender. The trick with surrender, however, is that God's being in charge does not free us of personal responsibility, choosing, or informed effort.

When we are good at many things, we need to learn surrender. I also learned about being authentic. It wasn't that I was so good at a lot of things; it was just that I only did the things that I did well. There's nothing wrong with that. I think it's a pretty good idea. Specialize in the things you do well. Surround yourself with those who know what you don't and let them do those things well. You just need to stay in touch with your intuitive and intellectual capacity enough to know when these others are wrong or not in alignment with your best judgment. You can always dabble in all the other things that interest you.

So there were the three marriages, and then, after letting go, I finally met my prince. After a long marriage (for me), he made his transition in 2000, and I am certain my new prince will arrive when it is time. Before that momentous event, there is *work* to occupy my time not necessarily a career or even a job. But this girl knows about *work*.

FOOD FOR THE *JOURNEY*

1. Can you let go, even of things that seem to be entirely your responsibility? Can you let them go to a Presence that is wiser, kinder, and stronger than you even if you can't see the end?
2. Can you shut your mouth, hold your peace, and trust that you are way more loved and powerful than you can imagine?
3. Are you willing, when things get rough or unpredictable, to hand over the outcome to a Higher Authority in your life?
4. This is a tough one that requires a lot of thought. "Is it safe to be you? Is it safe to be vulnerable?"
5. Can you list the ways it is not or has not been safe to be you? Are there or have there been times when being you just sucks? What did you learn in that space?

"Work is what I do best...and take detours, exits, rest stops..."
Lucy Shaw

I BE, I DO, I HAVE

When I was 9 years old, I had my very first job and can attest to the fact that I have not been without a work since. At 9, I began cleaning a house for a school teacher who lived down the street from us. She paid me $4.00 every Saturday to clean her house from top to bottom. To this day, when I smell Aero floor wax, I have this flood of memories of alternately putting wax on and taking wax off every other week in a house full of hardwood floors. It was bizarre. I would shine those floors up with that Aero wax only to come back two weeks later, take it off, and put on a new layer. Maybe she was just creating work for me, keeping the needy little 9-year-old working and encouraged.

I was so proud to be earning money because I wanted to contribute to my family's household. My mother was not always happy, and I thought that I if I helped her financially, it would make her happy. The first time I came home with that $4.00 and tried to give it to my mom, she got angry. She said, "Oh no. Don't you ever take your money and give it away like that. You worked for this money. This is your money. You get to use it. The only thing I ask is that you give me $1.00 to put away for you." She was always teaching. But then it felt like she was refusing to let me make her happy! My next job was at the neighborhood sundry store, followed by a job at the dry goods store. Then I had a job arranging flowers, followed by a job at the telephone company.

I cannot remember a time since I was 9 years old that I was without a job or work for longer than 6 months. It was my mother who insisted I know the difference between a job, a career, and work. Over the years, I have come to see them in an expanded and loose interpretation of my own. A job is when someone else pays you an amount of money around minimum wage, sets your time, and doesn't ask for a lot of creativity. You might get some conditional benefits.

A career is what you have when you can get paid above minimum wage, maybe call it a profession, get specialized training for it, have the possibility of getting promoted, and show up when people say you should or work under the illusion of being in charge of your time. You also get some conditional benefits.

What I call "Righteous Work" is when you can determine your own worth, hours, and pay based on your own work ethic, skills, creativity, and capacity to imagine. When this work is also your passion and you can truly do as much or as little as you want and still live with a sense of freedom, you are experiencing a joyful state of "Being." The conditional benefits become unconditional because you depend on a higher Source for them through a spiritually sustainable relationship with your Provider.

FOOD FOR THE *JOURNEY*

Did you know that most of us get focused on Doing, Having, and Being in that order? We believe that if we can just *do* enough, we can *have* enough and then we will *be* enough. I have learned that it actually works like this:

1. I BE. Before all else, like those Disciples, I need to get clarity on who I AM, whose I AM, and what all that means to me and for me. If this sounds too woo-woo for you, ask yourself about all of the times in your life that things worked out because you prayed (willfully or not) or they worked out and you have no idea what happened. Along with this comes clarity of how you are "being." Am I BEING strong, kind, intelligent, loving, grateful, forgiving, peaceful, beautiful, fair, creative, resilient, and resourceful? The list can go on and on with all the positive attributes you desire, but the fact is that "I BE" simply means that this is who and what I am, no matter what is going on around me. It's what I hold onto with confidence! All of my thinking and feeling comes from my knowing who I BE. When I don't feel so hot physically, emotionally, spiritually, or mentally, it just means I am not holding onto my "I BE" with confidence or I have chosen another reality about my "beingness" that is less than positive. This is not positive thinking either!

2. I DO. I cannot "do" anything except that which is according to my belief and conviction about who and what 'I BE' plain and simple. Every action flows from who and what I am "being" from moment-to-moment. This is why we can take 100% responsibility for what shows up in our lives. Our DOING is always in alignment with our BEING.

19

3. I am HAVING the life that resonates with the consistency of my being and doing. Whatever is going on in my life can always be adjusted via my state of BEING. So, in this moment, "What state of being are you experiencing?" I can be in the physical and intellectual State of Tennessee and in an emotional and spiritual state of abundance, peace, and happiness if I begin with I BE.

4. Working on the "I BE" part requires consistent discipline. When that part of us needs realignment, you can bet on getting in a place that feels like "STUCK."

"There is always a way to turn yourself into an asset." Lucy

I went to Gary, Indiana the summer after my first year in college to stay with an Aunt. I got a job working for a physician as a medical assistant. I knew nothing about how to be a medical assistant, so I called my mother to ask her what I should do. First, she admitted that she didn't have a clue what medical assistants did, either! She thought I should just make up my own job description, no matter what they thought they wanted. She reminded me that I knew how to type and wondered if anyone else in the office had gone to college or knew how to type. Ironically, no one there had either of these claims to fame. My mother's sage advice was this, "Look around, see what needs to be done, and do it before you are asked. Anticipate that Doctor and make yourself absolutely indispensable."

I was 19 years old, with 10 years of work experience under my belt, and while I had worthiness issues, working hard and smart was not an issue. Within two months, I was managing the office, making the bank deposits, driving the doctor's Jaguar to do errands, and totally enthralled with the idea of health and healing! I stayed in Gary, working for the doctor, got married, had my first child, got divorced, remarried, and took yet another detour on my *Journey*.

FOOD FOR THE *JOURNEY*

1. Look around. What skill do you possess that no one else seems to have? Perhaps it is the thing people always say to you, "I wish I could do that like you!" You don't think it's such a big deal because it comes easy to you and you take it for granted. Maybe this is your unique gift or talent. Maybe you can learn to appreciate and nurture it.

2. Are you willing to serve in such a way that someone feels life or work without you would be less easy, less structured, or less enjoyable? This does not mean you create an environment of dependency. Rather it is an environment of dependability.

GET A PIB!

"A hard head makes a soft behind." My Mama

"Therefore encourage one another and build one another up, just as you are doing." 1 Thessalonians 5:11 KJV

In the midst of a new bad marriage, I went to nursing school, feeling like it was time I got a career. I graduated nearly nine months pregnant. Again, my choice was not a good one. When this marriage broke up, I fled back home to Memphis and my mother's house with two small children. I began to work at what was one of the largest hospitals in the world at that time, and I think I was the third African-American registered nurse ever hired.

I was working three jobs. I was teaching high school during the day, a charge nurse on the three to eleven shift, and then on the weekends I was a home health nurse making emergency house calls. I was working all of these jobs to take care of my children, and frankly, get out of my mother's house. I met a man who was very helpful with my sons, married again for the wrong reasons, and if you are counting, at this point I was up to husband #3.

This was the divorce that led to my taking a leave of absence from the compulsion to be stuck on stupid; learn to trust God and begin to pay attention to creating a life I might love to live. Alas, for me it wasn't that simple. I believe I had to take some more detours, exits, and rest stops just so I could share *Journeys* with others in ways that matter.

There's a wonderful poem by Langston Hughes, the great African-American poet, titled *Mother to Son*. The mother says to the son, "life for me ain't been no crystal stair." The mother is talking to him, giving him advice, and she talks about climbing the ladder of success, that you need to keep going no matter what happens, and that while life for her "ain't been no crystal stair," she keeps on climbing the staircase.

She describes the staircase as having splinters and tacks, torn boards, and places without carpet. Sometimes she reaches a landing to find that there is no light or has to turn corners in the dark and even walk in the dark for long periods of time. But her advice to the boy is "don't turn back."

I like to think that I have been shaped by the *Journey* of life, which is often like this mother's rugged staircase. Yet I do know from experience that there are many times in between where the staircase is indeed crystal and everything is good. However, when it is truly time to go higher, when it's time to get off the crystal staircase and rough it for a while, we have to be willing to do that. The key is to remember that it is still a staircase and we can still choose to go *up*. This idea became my life's motto, "Okay, I'm getting off the crystal stair for a new lesson."

"Is it time for an Exit, a detour, or a rest stop? Whatever, it's time for a change of thinking and feeling." Lucy

When the staircase is no longer crystal, when the thrill is gone and the passion is stagnant, I think of it as standing under a great big exit sign that you don't see because you won't look up. It's time to take a rest, take a detour (or whatever helps you figure out what the next lesson might be), prepare to receive the blessing inherent in it, choose the right exit ramp, and get on a new road. I have had many life experiences and made mistakes that have helped me to know the signs.

Standing still on the exit ramp, not knowing which way to go is scary. Sometimes you don't know if it's the speed that frightens you or the not knowing that it's the right exit or all those horns blowing urging you on and making you feel stupid for hesitating. Sometimes it's the fear of changing directions and being judged for having possibly made a mistake with the last choice. And then there are the feelings of defeat and mistrusting your own judgment, intentions, and motivations.

But here is what I know. It is necessary for you to STOP, get help, ask the right questions, and expect the right answers to start showing up. In my practice, I am blessed with a connection to Spirit that provides the intuitive impetus to help my clients. When I am prayed up (intentionally surrendered and focused on being of service) ideas, answers, direction, and active compassion that I could never have planned for shows up. Within the realm of grace and intuition, answers for my clients show up, sometimes as a new technique for focus and setting intention; a book from my shelf; other people or connections; new and untried experiences that the client has avoided; questions that go straight to the heart of the matter; and always an expansion of their capacity to think into bigger, better, more life-affirming possibilities.

Sometimes we just need a Partner in Believing, a *PIB*. I learned this concept from Mary Morrisey, from whom I received my initial Life Coaching certification. I have since expanded this concept into one of my own most significant tools for supporting clients. When I experienced one of my darkest nights of the soul, I did not have a *PIB*. I had no one I could trust with my fears and perceived vulnerabilities. How do you know when you need your own *PIB*?

FOOD FOR THE *JOURNEY*

You need a Partner in Believing when there are things you cannot do adequately for yourself because of fear, you don't know how, anxiety, lack of trust, or not having a clue for how to get unstuck. Or maybe you just want help with organizing and pursuing your dream!

1. You need someone to pray with you, for you.
2. You need someone who can believe for you when you cannot believe for yourself.
3. You need someone to bring you back to center and into right now.

4. You need someone to dream with you, to be curious, to encourage you.
5. You need someone to support you in 'becoming', without taking away your 100% responsibility for the outcome.
6. You need someone to remind you of the Truth about who you BE.

There are many more functions of a Partner in Believing. A mature, spiritually grounded, and committed Coach can offer this wonderful support, while allowing you to learn how to be your own Guru!

"Therefore we do not lose heart. Though outwardly we are wasting away, yet inwardly we are being renewed day by day. For our light and momentary troubles are achieving for us an eternal glory that far outweighs them all. So we fix our eyes not on what is seen, but on what is unseen, since what is seen is temporary, but what is unseen is eternal."

2Corinthians 4: 16-18

STUCK!

"I AM STANDING STILL, SCARED TO GO, SCARED TO STAY...IT JUST FEELS LIKE I AM STUCK! " A Client

This is such an awful feeling to have, especially if your life has been all about success and failure does not seem to be an option. This is a lot like the addict, who finds himself at a do or die point. In Alcoholics Anonymous, Step 1 reads: "We admitted we were powerless over alcohol, that our lives have become unmanageable."

I have a friend who is a Drug and Substance Abuse Therapist. He tells me that we all have some sort of recognized or un-recognized addiction. The Latin derivative of the word 'addictio' is a giving-over or surrender to something. In this instance, I might agree with him that being stuck can be like an insidious, crippling, and controlling addiction. It can also morph into a surrender to something in us that is so much less than the greater expectations we hold for ourselves. This is what I hear my clients describe when they voice feelings of being stuck and unable to control the fear of the unknown or what they cannot understand; the anxiety this produces, and the feelings of being someone they don't like or don't want to be. Worst of all is the feeling of surrendering their power to something or someone wiser in order to move into something better, new, and unknown. This brings with it feelings of anger and inadequacy that have to be processed.

> **However, when we are stuck is not the time to be sacrificial. This is the time to put yourself first! There is a powerful instruction to "Love your neighbor as yourself." Some of us have been confused by that and interpret it as the need to put others first. I know from hard earned experience that it is a call to know whose we are, who we are, and to love ourselves deeply enough that it becomes possible to love another.**

It also requires compassion for self and others that acknowledges our shared humanity. I recently talked to an attorney, who said that as a single person, she has taken to assuming that every new date has his own "emotional deal-breakers." So to save time, she just asks them, "So what is your emotional deal-breaker? Tell me yours and I will tell you mine." Some examples are: bad grammar, poor driving skills, unkempt beards, dirty fingernails, being late, and unkept promises. The list can be long, seemingly silly, and idiosyncratic! Being stuck is like being in an emotional deal-breaker loop that causes us to be hyper-critical of ourselves and everyone else.

When we get stuck, chances are we have been in this particular place before. The ones that last longer are the ones we don't quickly admit to and do something about. Sometimes, we just forget that we've been here before and don't remember what we did the last time to escape. We imagine that this experience will just magically go away. When it doesn't, we go deeper, feel less and less in control, and love ourselves less and less.

And here I have said nothing about the impact all of this may have on those closest to us! Yet, it is those closest to us that we sometimes shift our focus to instead of ourselves. Why? Successful people sometimes have a tendency to rescue everybody, but themselves. Also, it's a great and useful distraction. However, when we are stuck is not the time to be sacrificial. This is the time to put yourself first! There is a powerful instruction to "Love your neighbor as yourself." Some of us have been confused by that and interpret it as the need to put others first. I know from hard earned experience that it is a call to know whose we are, who we are, and to love ourselves deeply enough that it becomes possible to love another.

Now be careful that you don't take what I have said in this section as an accusation that being stuck means you have an addiction! However, like an addiction, being stuck is a call to a new level of discipline.

1. Like my therapist friend would say, look for the symptomatology. How are you feeling? Powerless, unable to make a move, scared, ashamed? Worst case scenario, it might feel like you have simply lost the ability to effectively manage your decisions and choices. This feels terrible to a person accustomed to being the "go-to" person for others!

2. Admit there is a problem.

3. Is this one of your routine "emotional deal-breakers" that has morphed into something else? Remember that you have been here before and that you came out of it before and you can do it again.

4. Get some trusted help! Don't be ashamed. You are an awesome piece of goodness and you are being led to something bigger and better. You just need some guidance over the rough terrain.

5. Let go! Stop obsessing about it and start being thankful for the relentless urge to change direction in your life.

QUARTER-MOON THINKING©

"Now faith is the substance of things hoped for, the evidence of things not seen." Hebrews 11:1 KJV

Buttercup: We'll never survive.

Westley: Nonsense. You're only saying that because no one ever has.

From the movie: *The Princess Bride,* 1987

Could it be that sometimes, when we are stuck, we are actually having a crisis of faith? Or maybe we are having a bloody episode of scarcity thinking and find that we have been taken prisoner. I don't particularly like the language "scarcity thinking" or "impoverished thinking." I know it rightfully denotes the idea that there are behaviors that come out of our belief that there is <u>not enough</u>. I lean towards a bit more compassionate way of thinking about it. Perhaps my thinking doesn't change the reality of the behavior, but it does provide a different way of considering how these behaviors come to be.

Imagine you live in a land where the only moon you ever see is a quarter moon. This is your reality. Along comes someone who has seen all eight phases of the moon including a big, round full one! Your reality, or perhaps your bias, is that your experience has made you a quarter-moon thinker.

For you, moons are never bigger or smaller than the quarter moon, whether it is waning or waxing. That full-moon thinker challenges you to consider so many more possibilities. You are being challenged to believe that a full moon is possible even if you never saw one! In fact, he may tell you that there is even a crescent moon, smaller than the quarter moon! Then, he may go so far as to tell you that these phases of the moon can influence the tides and maybe even your behavior. But here is the crux of the matter how can one hope for something never seen or experienced?

One of the chief causes of money problems, overwork, misguided ambition, lack of ambition, overspending, fears of spending, earning or saving, and worth have to do with Quarter-Moon vs Full-Moon Thinking. When we are stuck, one of our biggest threats resonates around our beliefs about money and motivation. We do not live in vacuums so we are subject to all that goes on around us, including the mass thoughts and opinions of others. We end up asking ourselves, "What about my livelihood?" It's hard to honor our curiosity or passion when we think it might interfere with our capacity to make a living!

One of the most important tasks I give my clients is the one of testing for Quarter-Moon Thinking. While I have many ways for testing and repairing this thinking, here is something to consider. Quarter-Moon Thinking has a voice of constriction. Full-Moon Thinking is always the voice that urges us to expand.

- The voice of expansion often says:
  - I can...
  - I will...
  - I have the power to choose-then declare...
  - I choose...
- The voice of constriction often says:
  - I can't...
  - I won't...
  - I don't know how...
  - I don't have the power to choose...

Improvement of the human condition hinges on faith, vision, and imagination.

Improvement of the human condition hinges on faith, vision, and imagination. Moving forward and maintaining forward momentum is an act of these three attributes. Sometimes, successful people will sacrifice their happiness for the biased voice of Quarter-Moon Thinking, even when they have been exposed to or have practiced and received the

33

benefits of Full-Moon Thinking. The Coach's work is to remind you of these abilities. Moreover, my work is to help you uncover the hidden beliefs and biases that seemingly pop up out of nowhere and force you into change.

FOOD FOR THE *JOURNEY*

1. Which voice are you listening to, the voice of Expansion or Constriction?
2. Can you walk around in a spirit of Gratitude for being reminded of the need to question the voice?
3. Are you willing to not only say thank you to that voice of constriction for revealing itself, but to also tell the voice that you love it, you are so sorry, ask its forgiveness, and let it go? It is your teacher and needs to be set free.
4. Are you willing to exercise the freedom to CHOOSE? Sometimes, the easiest way to break the spell of being stuck is to simply choose expansion over constriction.

IMAGINATION AND VISION

"And the LORD answered me, and said, write the vision, and make it plain upon tables, that he may run that readeth it." Habakkuk 2:2 KJV

"Imagination is the only weapon in the war against reality." The Cheshire Cat, *Alice in Wonderland*

One of the hardest concepts to take hold of is the Cosmic Law of Cause and Effect. We minimize this particular Law by limiting it to things that we can see, touch, hear, smell, and taste in the physical realm. Yet, in the hands of someone with discipline and understanding it becomes exceedingly powerful. There are many more cosmic laws and they are all worth learning about. They all seem to resonate around our power as creative thinkers; that awesome ability we possess to imagine the life we have in present and future terms.

We are continually creating our own life experiences with our thoughts as mind-pictures, and attaching more or less powerful emotions to give those pictures added momentum. Then we move around (or run around), unconsciously feeding the vision and act totally surprised when the vision shows up as facts in our lives.

Here is an example from my own life. Several years ago, I got the distinct desire to buy a new car. My husband always had a Mercedes, while I preferred a Cadillac. I have learned to listen to the voice of expansion, the voice of God, and I believe God's will for me is always good. So as I was riding down the street with the intention of going to the Cadillac dealer to select my next vehicle, I passed the Mercedes dealership. When I got ready to turn into the Cadillac dealership, I had this really strong urge to turn around and go to the Mercedes place.

I followed the push, although reluctantly. All the while, I was having this running dialogue with what I call "The Voice" about how I did not want the expensive upkeep or my perceived "flash" of a Mercedes. Relenting, I looked and found a Mercedes I liked, but I was unable to get the deal I wanted (another way of blocking my blessing). Still, The Voice persisted and I called my nephew, who is a dealer, and he sourced the perfect Mercedes for the perfect price. I took possession of the car and it was such a cool ride! However, for the first week I had it, I began to notice that I felt anxious whenever I drove it. I was careful about what I wore (dressing down), careful where I went (trying to be inconspicuous), and just not truly embracing the car as being right for me or me as being ready or worthy of it.

The car was very low to the ground and on the fifth day of possession, a Thursday, I parked in a hotel lot and bent the front fender on a concrete parking stop. I called a repair shop and was told I could bring it in the next day. I decided to wait until Monday, as I was expecting house guests that weekend. I went to bed on Friday night and slept like a log.

Saturday morning, I awakened to what had been one of the worst storms and floods in the history of Memphis. I had parked the car at the back of the house. My lot is lower in the back than in the front. By the time I awakened, the water had begun to recede, but my car had been drowned! It was dead and would never start again because the electrical system in it was destroyed. I remember standing beside it, lamenting its death and thinking, "This is what happens when you reject a gift and don't love it enough to take it for repair." And right on the heels of that thought was that I could now get my Cadillac and be comfortable.

Our deepest fear is not that we are inadequate. Our deepest fear is that we are powerful beyond measure.

So what do I think really happened?

- My husband, who had died, was a larger-than-life person. He was able to command a room just by showing up; loved big, beautiful cars; and never saw money as an obstruction to having anything he desired.

- In spite of all of my teaching and learning, I still had unresolved issues about money, spending, and worthiness. (Albeit, I never had a problem spending on beautiful clothes.) I also still hated being flashy, being the center of attention, or being talked about! And I was super good at hiding my fears for the sake of getting the job done, whatever it might be.

- I had always silently and ashamedly resented my husband's ability to be so free and confident when it came to money, spending, and letting his big, awesome light shine.

- I was a victim of the well-stated Marianne Williamson quote, "Our deepest fear is not that we are inadequate. Our deepest fear is that we are powerful beyond measure. It is our light, not our darkness that most frightens us. We ask ourselves, who am I to be brilliant, gorgeous, talented, and fabulous? Actually, who are you *not* to be? You are a child of God. Your playing small does not serve the world. There is nothing enlightened about shrinking so that other people won't feel insecure around you. We are all meant to shine, as children do. We were born to make manifest the glory of God that is within us. It's not just in some of us; it's in everyone. And as we let our own light shine, we unconsciously give other people permission to do the same. As we are liberated from our own fear, our presence automatically liberates others." Marianne

Williamson, *A Return To Love: Reflections on the Principles of A Course in Miracles*, Harper Collins, 1992. From Chapter 7, Section 3 (Pg. 190-191). **I wanted to allow others to shine, but could only take so much light for myself!**

It seems as if this story is not about imagining, having a vision, making it plain, and running with it. Actually, it is. Many successful people have great plans, goals, and visions for their lives, but often our own plans are sabotaged by our capacity to truly receive the things we believe we want.

This experience for me was the opportunity to learn that I cannot have anything that I am not willing to receive. It also means that I can never begin my dialogue with a client at the point of vision. Our individual thinking and feelings can trump the realization of any dream we may have for ourselves. This was grace working for me, and when grace is at work, things can go really fast to be sure that we get both the lesson and the blessing. For me, the lesson was that there is power in listening to The Voice; The Voice is always right even when it seems wrong. More importantly, I desperately needed to get rid of my last vestiges of unworthiness and fear of being a person of light. Had I not done so, I could not be the Coach that I am.

Here is something to ponder. There are "facts" and then there is the TRUTH. The Truth is that which IS; it is eternally sustained by all of the universal laws of this world. Facts are what we believe to be reality and this reality is always changing. This reality keeps us trapped in fears and unbelief in limitless possibilities. The Truth is that we are all made to shine period. The test is our ability to believe it, envision it, and make it plain not just by writing it on paper, but inscribing it on the screens of our minds and enriching it with feelings of love, not fear. When we have done this, we are able to "run with it." How do we run with it? We go about our lives as if our vision is already reality. This is the power of the "graven image."

Oh, and by the way, my insurance company immediately had my destroyed car picked up and issued a check for the full value of the vehicle. The fair market price exceeded what I paid for it and I was blessed according to the promise, "pressed down, shaken together, and running over." Can you see how the blessing went beyond the money?

FOOD FOR THE *JOURNEY*

1. Do you have a big, bad, bodacious dream? Does it have some "Yes, buts…" attached to it? If so, you had better work on those buts.
2. Have you dared to imagine yourself walking in that dream, living it, and having it? Boldly and right now?
3. When you envision yourself living the life in that dream, what does it feel, smell, look, taste, and sound like?
4. What does the person having this dream think, say, and feel?
5. Are you BEING that person NOW?

WILL THIS WORK FOR YOU

"Above all else, guard your heart, for it is the wellspring of life" Proverbs 4:23, NIV

"Keep thy heart with all diligence; for out of it are the issues of life." KJV

My clients are people who have already experienced success in a career, lifestyle, or relationship. Many already have a strong faith ideology or practice. But because we are on planet Earth, in Earth University to learn and to grow; movement from one grade or class to another is not optional. My beloved clients often show up in pain. It is usually a significant pain of the heart that won't let go. They speak of getting a personal vibe that "I'm not doing what I ought to be doing" or "I'm not doing enough of it" or "I've lost my passion, and I just need somebody to help me get unstuck. I have tried all that I know how to do and it's not working for me anymore."

Then again, clients are referred by past clients or spouses who have experienced a *Journey* with me. Sometimes, the client is referred by their employer. The boss recognizes their worth to the firm, has noticed a change in work quality, and wants to salvage or rescue the employee. And then, there are clients who don't so much describe what they feel as pain, but rather a nagging longing or a discontent.

No matter how my client finds me, he or she is smart, motivated, ambitious, kind, and values personal and professional achievement. I have never once had a client who lacked motivation, a kindness of heart, or an unwillingness to move to another level of cognitive, behavioral, and emotional competence. My work is to be a Partner in Believing or PIB. My work is to help the client recognize that they are so much more than whatever their present experience in life is; to help them find out what that might look like and to fall in love with outrageous possibilities. At the same time, he/she must walk the perilous line of learning to love where he/she has already been, to love the person who went there, and uncover all the fantastic gifts and talents that have sustained him/her up to the present.

Most of all, I'm trying to get my client unstuck and back to a place of neutrality. What I really want to see them do is figure out that being stuck is not a bad thing. 'Stuck' is just the intersection or the co-incidence of their longing and their discontent. Between these two things, we long to do something new on the one hand, and on the other hand, we're terribly unhappy with something in our present lives. In the middle of that is the Call.

It's the Call to be moved into a bigger, better, fuller, more successful, and more satisfied state of BEING. It's the Call to take the leap from one grade level to another. Sometimes the leap or move is sideways, so we can learn the other side of our present circumstances. Sometimes, we have to go back to the prior grade level to review, appreciate, or refresh previous lessons. When clients are finished with me, they have tools that help them to identify and be propelled into the space they not only want to go to, but that their heart is begging for.

And that brings us to the two iterations of Proverbs 4:23. In one version, we are told to **"Above all else, guard your heart, for it is the wellspring of life."** The heart is where our desires, emotions, and motives live. Here we are being told that the most important thing we can ever do is pay attention to what is going on in that part of us. When our desires, emotions, and motives are less than satisfactory to our well-being, it will show up as a negative impact on our capacity to create!

Then the second version says, **"Keep thy heart with all diligence; for out of it are the issues of life."** Again, I think that "diligence" begs the need to relentlessly pay attention and do something about all of the "issues" that show up, simply because we are not being disciplined, focused, and intentional. You got issues? Consider this verse.

I think we all have basically the same purpose here on earth, but we actualize it differently. We all have our unique ways of doing the thing we came here to do. Sometimes, maybe the way that we're doing what we need to do is no longer working for us or it doesn't excite us. My intention with clients is to help them get to where they love themselves, get unstuck, and learn how to transform that self-love into love and appreciation for others.

Learning and working with the law of circulation provides a competency in giving AND receiving over and over. This means that when we make money or gain resources, our intention and purpose includes making others' lives better right along with ours. This implies a working knowledge of the power of gratitude. I like to see the light bulbs flash as the person falls in love with themselves sometimes for the first time ever. Whatever that looks like for the client is most important. I don't already know what it looks like, but I help them figure it out.

Pain is a tricky thing. It can hide behind so many disguises. Something hurts my client, so my first job is always to uncover the nature of the pain. Where does it hurt? Does it hurt in the spirit? Does it hurt in the mind? Is it an intellectual failure? Does it just hurt in your very heart and soul? Are you hurting physically? I have to find the hurt, and then address the hurt. It may simply be a soft, slow, nagging hurt, but it is still unpleasantness felt in some part of the client's being. Many of my clients come not wanting to admit to any form of pain. That's okay because at some point in the *Journey* the pain will show itself because its purpose is to move you to another place.

I know this to be true from personal experience. When I have ignored my brokenness, the pain of it would not stop until it got some attention. The pain may first show up in my dreams, denying me the gift of sleep. When that doesn't work, it becomes an emotional pain that shows up as uncommon or irrational behavior. If I ignore that, it will proceed to the organ or part of my body most suited for getting my attention through physical pain. We are so "wonderfully and fearfully made," and each part of us works to support the "all" of us in faithful and relentless ways.

We are wired for greatness!

We are wired for greatness! If you have the courage to work on learning how to live a life that you love, instead of one that you are just making do with, then I'm the girl to see. If you want to find tools for finding, maintaining, and sustaining balance in your life, I'm the girl. What people really come to me for is to find balance, to find and renew their purpose, to find and renew their passion, and to do something in the world that makes a difference. What we want does not have to be big, famous, or show-stopping. There is nothing wrong with big, famous, or show-stopping. Whatever your gift, talent, and purpose is, there is no peace until it is acknowledged and allowed to flourish.

FOOD FOR THE *JOURNEY*

Answering the following questions may help you know that you could benefit from a *Journey* coaching experience.

1. I am so discontent with the _____ in my life.
2. I yearn for _____ in my life.
3. I wish I had someone to help me with this without judgment, criticism, or blame.
4. My relationships, career, or money is at risk.
5. I am smart, usually kind, ambitious, and know what happiness and success feels like.
6. I so want to fall in love with ME and appreciate ME.
7. I already have a tool box; I just need to sharpen those I have and collect a few more.

LEARNING TO LIVE IN THE NEXUS

"The LORD God took the man and put him in the Garden of Eden to work it and take care of it." Genesis 2:15 NIV

"When you don't cover up the world with words and labels, a sense of the miraculous returns to your life that was lost a long time ago when humanity, instead of using thought, became possessed by thought."
— Eckhart Tolle, A New Earth: Awakening to Your Life's Purpose

What I'm usually trying to do is share tools for living in the Nexus. I use an infinity sign to create an image of life as a finite experience in an unlimited field of possibilities. The infinity sign itself goes along an axis and it winds, going one way, and then the other. But there is the point called the Nexus where the paths intersect and cross over. To me, that Nexus is the NOW.

Throughout the day, we're going back and forth. We're going to the past, we're going to the future, and we forget that the past is gone, and today, this moment, is the only time we have to create tomorrow. I can choose to live in my "NOW," accepting the impermanence of life in a way that helps me to not be so attached to how things turn out. I can learn how to keep it neutral by refusing to name the experience either good or bad. The key is to govern my own expectations.

NOW is really all we have. NOW is neutral. We get to name it and react or respond to it. And more important, we get to create *in* it. It is our own personal Garden that we are required to tend. In tending it, we get to name everything in the field. This, however, requires the discipline of faith, conviction, and contentment. Sometimes, things don't seem to grow like we want them to. Sometimes, we think we planted one thing only to see something different come up. Even if we go from one side of the Nexus to the other, we still must return to the NOW and meet the temptation to name it good or bad.

I remember having a person in my life who I labeled a "thorn in my side." I was so focused on what he had done to me in the past that was hurtful and what I wanted to happen to him in the future that the rage and anger did indeed create a pain in the region of my liver in my side. I had many opportunities to name my experiences with him as powerless, nothing, a lesson, or a blessing, but I chose to use my time going from side-to-side in the field of infinite possibilities, naming him a problem. The capacity to name or "speak a thing and have it so" is pretty powerful! It was not until I stood still with intention and expressed Gratitude whenever I thought of him that I was able to get rid of my pain and let go of all that he had previously meant to me. Then, and only by choosing, was I able to go UP instead of down or side-to-side.

The greatest gift we have is the one we call "free will." My clients learn that a better definition of "will" is "choice."

The greatest gift we have is the one we call "free will." My clients learn that a better definition of "will" is "choice." No one can ever take away our power to choose; and intentionally, consciously, or neither, we are always choosing. When I speak or teach about poverty, one of the concepts is that a person in generational poverty often appears to not have power, choice, or a future story.

While this may seem to be a fact to the person in that experience, the Truth is that we all have power, choice, and a future story as a gift and promise from God. What we do not all experience is the conscious opportunity to learn how to access the gifts within ourselves. This is the benefit of having the right Coach, as being stuck is often a form of "poverty of the spirit." The Bible and other Wisdom writings tell us that "the poor in spirit will always be with us." But we are also given a multitude of ways to escape!

We learn very early in life how to be unhappy. We learn to judge, criticize, and condemn others. We learn from *others* how to judge, criticize, and condemn ourselves far better than anyone else can.

Living in the Nexus requires tools for Focus. One of these is prayer. I read recently that prayer and meditation is no more than focus with intention or 'intentional focus'. Again, this is a form of necessary discipline. Some clients have none, some have misguided focus, and some are addicted to multi-tasking and avoiding focus. But as I said more than once in the previous chapter, happiness is a product of PAYING ATTENTION, FOCUS. Focus is also known as Mindfulness.

One of my tools for focus is the Heart Box. The client gets a little booklet and a box filled with multi-colored pebbles. He/she is given an assignment to perform a task in ten minutes. I have rarely had anyone take ten minutes to complete the task. Instead, most people finish in 3-5 minutes when they first do the exercise. I assign this for three weeks, twice a day. Living in the Nexus is like this. Being present requires focus, concentration, intention, contentment, and a willingness to do nothing! It especially requires that we let go of the pesky need to think and admire our problem-solving skills, or lack thereof.

Another essential tool for Living in the Nexus is learning how to bring oneself back to zero, or the Nexus, in terms of our emotions. Among a few other Energy Medicine practices, I use Emotional Freedom Technique (EFT or Tapping). Often, it is our unruly, overbearing fears that take us over the edge and steal our peace. For some clients, this is a welcome and intuitive tool. For others, I have to find other methods. However, managing emotions is a must for balance.

I also try to help my clients find something bigger than themselves, outside of themselves; a spiritual anchor. I don't teach religion. I just help the client understand the power of the spirit, and that when body, mind, and spirit are not in sync one of them is going to rebel. Sometimes they all rebel, like they did with me when I hit rock bottom. Pertinent to living in the Nexus is the capacity to pay attention to the physical body. When you begin to understand the symptomatology that comes out of the body, it will lead you right back to what's going on in your head, your spirit, or your heart.

For example, I had a client with really bad gall bladder attacks, and she looked like perhaps the most humble, pleasant person you ever met. But there's a funny thing about the gall bladder and the liver. This is where we process anger and rage or things you feel made "to swallow." If you suppress it, you're going to end up making little angry stones, or you're just going to have that terrible shoulder pain. You're going to have pain that refers from your gall bladder up to your shoulder.

What I like to do with my clients, is to help them understand that a lot of symptomatology in the physical body is just the spirits' way of getting rid of some emotions that are not conducive to overall health. My mother died of liver disease and was never a drinker of alcohol! But what she did do was stuff down a lot of rage and resentment that came from living with my dad.

Growth is a law of the universe. Recently, I tried the white vinegar treatment for the weeds in the cracks of my driveway. Maybe I didn't keep it up like I should have, but in two weeks they were all back, pushing up through those cracks with a vengeance. Even weeds got the memo for *Life*! Expansion and growth is a universal imperative. If you don't cooperate with it, if you don't do the things you need to do, all sorts of awful things start to happen.

On the other hand, when we develop an understanding and have a tool set that we actually put to use, we get to see beautiful things grow in our field of possibilities. I can just say to people, "It's okay that you don't do this now. You just need to know that the universe is set up to get your attention and force you to grow. If you're not growing, you're quite possibly dying. We are here to grow!"

FOOD FOR THE *JOURNEY*

Can you answer yes to these with specificity?

1. Do you have a daily focus, prayer, mindfulness, or intentionality ritual?

2. Do you have a way to bring yourself into the present when you stray and get stuck in the past or the future.

3. Do you have something or someone in your life analogous to "a thorn in the side," "a pain in the butt," or maybe "an albatross around your neck?" If so, how is that pain in your side, those hemorrhoids, or that stiff and painful neck working for you?

A FEW NECESSITIES FOR THE
JOURNEY

"For which of you, desiring to build a tower, does not first sit down and count the cost, whether he has enough to complete it?" Luke 14:28 ESV

"Learn to get in touch with the silence within yourself, and know that everything in life has purpose. There are no mistakes, no coincidences, all events are blessings given to us to learn from." Elisabeth Kubler-Ross

When I take a client, there are things that we both need to do before the choice is made to work together. Then there are choices along the way that make for a smooth *Journey*.

In my initial interview with a client, I am looking for a comfortable fit. First and foremost, I need to feel like we are compatible enough to "build a tower." And just like that scriptural quote, we are either building a tower out of a place you want to leave or a tower to the place you want to go. If I mention God, a Higher Power, Wisdom Books, or the Bible do you cringe? When I explain to you the "why" of referring to these, do you get okay? Is it okay that we talk about things of the spirit and definitely leave religious choices up to you?

I look for physical and emotional signs of distress. I look for your pain. I look for your longings and discontent and your willingness to talk about them. And I look for your willingness to pay the cost both literally and figuratively. Are you willing to see yourself as deserving of this financial investment in yourself? Moreover, are you willing to invest the time and focus needed to learn new ways of being or to let go of old ways that no longer serve you?

I want to know if you have tried a Coaching relationship before. How did that work out for you? I also want to know a little about your worldview. How do you view mistakes, pain, opportunity, and choice?

One of the big concerns for me is the client's willingness to take 100% responsibility for their own role in the success of the *Journey*. I will hold him/her accountable and provide support, but the real work is done by the individual.

From my own level of responsibility, the very first thing that's important, even in our preliminary interview, is that I make a strong effort to never go into a session without doing what I need to do to be 100% present with intention. My intention is not to sacrifice myself for my client, but I need to be so clear to myself that I am not going in just to give, but also to receive. When I look at that person, I am seeing someone who has graciously allowed me to go on this leg of their life's *Journey* with them, and that's an honor and a privilege. I have to receive the gift they came to bring me, as well. It is a profound and sacred honor to get to go on a *Journey* with somebody, and so I need to make sure that I'm all in, all there, and ready to both give and receive.

Then the next thing, of course, is to be certain that I model the behavior that I have learned allows my client to be receptive to new ideas and ways of learning and doing. It's like the testimony at the beginning of the book where Lori said, "Wow, you were so patient. You were so available." All of those kinds of behaviors must be habitual for me. When you are the boss, or when you are a successful person, you're always giving to other people, so one of the things that you are hungry for when you get into a coaching relationship is having someone who will give to you, who will attend to you in a respectful and caring way without any expectations other than mutual growth.

I expect my clients to read! Reading requires focus and discipline. There are certainly different learning styles and some people are Kinesthetic (needing to touch and handle things), while others are Auditory and learn best by listening. This mix will be provided. Learning how to be still, learning how to be focused is really a challenge for a lot of people. Yet concentration and focus is a major skill that has been lost in our present educational system. Reading for understanding and contemplative skill is an underestimated advantage in our present world and is not likely to be an asset that passes away.

I once had a Chairman of the Board of the hospital who had two favorite statements. The first he attributed to Thomas Jefferson, and I have not been able to verify that, but here is what my Chairman said, "We *govern* a nation of educated people and *rule* a nation of un-educated people." Another statement attributed to Jefferson, but also not validated is, "An educated citizenry is a vital requisite for our survival as a free people."

While I may not be one of Thomas Jefferson's biggest fans; like him I do love the idea of freedom. And the *Journey* is all about helping myself and the client identify just what freedom means to them. For me, Freedom is the capacity to be, do, and have joy and abundance in my life; expressing this freedom spiritually, mentally, and emotionally within my relationships and my finances. I think this is evolutionary and changes just as we grow and change. Yet it is our commitment to studying for ourselves and owning and using what we know to attain, maintain, and sustain freedom for ourselves and others that takes us higher and higher.

"It takes forty years to be forty."

The second quote from the Chairman was, "It takes forty years to be forty." It took me a while to get his meaning, but the truth is that it takes as long as it takes to complete a *Journey* into and through change. While the *Journey* with my clients is an initial seven-week engagement, its success is dependent upon both my commitment and the client's. The client is always free to commit to as many rounds as desired.

As you have already heard, learning to manage and own feelings and emotions is a big requirement. Journaling works for some. I give my clients books according to things that come up. I may give them, Caroline Myss' wonderful CD on Self-Esteem. In spite of being successful, self-worth is a big issue. One of the ways that people turn out to be successful is that they had a parent or somebody who pushed them. The way they pushed them was by repeatedly saying, "That's not good enough. Do it again." This is the chief way we learn negative self-talk, and that's how we then push ourselves. We really have to undo that skill.

In a nutshell, much of my work with clients is unique because it is intuitive, and therefore, very personalized. While some things are common to every *Journey*, each route is still unique to individual needs, dreams, and desires.

FOOD FOR THE *JOURNEY*

1. I am willing to read and study something that I may have never considered learning before.

2. I deserve to invest in my life with money and time, just for my own personal growth.
3. I am willing to take 100% responsibility for what is and what can show up in my life!

AVOIDING FAILURE ON THE *JOURNEY*

"Let your passion be the reason for your existence and your successes the product of your persistence." - www.dailyquotes.com

"God crowns the humble with victory." Psalms 149:4

The ultimate path to failure seems to me to show up as an inability to commit to being 100% responsible for whatever shows up in our lives. This is manifest in constant whining, blame, guilt, anger, and resentment. When people come, not ready to assume that responsibility, they're not going to make it to the next blessing awaiting them. Their effort will be half-hearted. When I select clients, I won't choose to work with somebody when I can pick up on those things that tell me they aren't really ready. This shows up as not wanting to do the work or wanting me to do the work for them. I don't do the work for my clients.

So the first thing is an assessment of your willingness to get to 100% readiness to take 100% responsibility for the outcomes in your life and to grow. Lack of readiness means it's just not time and we are not a good fit. No judgment, no criticism. It simply is not time. Some people demonstrate that they don't want to grow simply because they won't do the assignments. I might give somebody a simple assignment, like keeping a gratitude journal. If you show up and tell me, "Oh I didn't have time," well you're not ready. You just aren't ready. This has not become a priority for you. If you don't do the assignment because of the fear of what it might bring up, that's different.

The other thing is when I have somebody who really, really resists falling in love with themselves.
This may mean that their issues may be beyond the skills of a Life Coach. This person may be more suitable for a relationship with a licensed therapist. A pre-requisite to success and happiness is the capacity to acknowledge something greater than oneself, try to love that Presence, and then to love ourselves.

I have found that if I misjudge in this area, I am likely to have to spend my time on no other task but helping the client to begin the *Journey* into loving themselves and making the *choice* to love themselves. It is not the worst use of my time but certainly not the best. There are people trained in this who do it quite well, along with some other skills that I don't hold myself out as having. On the other hand, sometimes we just have a need to learn how to have some self-compassion. And looking at mine and my client's ability to suffer with their own humanity is one of the first things we do on the *Journey*. Self-Compassion is the doorway to compassion for others and to meaningful relationships.

As another method to avoid failure, I like for people to understand that in whatever they are doing, there needs to be something in it for others, not just themselves. A key question in all of our efforts is, "How will this help someone other than you?"

No matter what you call your higher power, if you don't want to acknowledge that there's something bigger than you out there that is making this world operate, you're going to have a hard time because where do you go for the ultimate comfort? Something's got to be bigger than you. I don't want to be anybody's guru.

However, I do want to guide you into being your own Guru and the CEO of your own life. Yet we do have to remember that like any CEO we need a good Board of Directors and a super powerful Chairman of the Board!

> Taking the *Journey* is an exercise in humility. To do that, to trust your most painful vulnerabilities to another, requires that you are humble and that the person with whom you share can demonstrate a deep appreciation for your courage. My own humility must come through as a willingness to see myself in your struggles and your triumphs. Lord knows, I have had plenty experience in both!

Taking the *Journey* is an exercise in humility. To do that, to trust your most painful vulnerabilities to another, requires that you are humble and that the person with whom you share can demonstrate a deep appreciation for your courage. My own humility must come through as a willingness to see myself in your struggles and your triumphs. Lord knows, I have had plenty experience in both!

FOOD FOR THE *JOURNEY* - *Look out for the "yes, but's..."*

1. I am willing to persist in whatever route I take to create and live the life I deserve and can love to live.
2. I am willing to fall deeply in love with myself so that I know what that looks and feels like and how it makes me better at loving others.

3. Even now, I can think of three ways taking the *Journey* will benefit someone other than me.

A FEW MORE PITFALLS TO AVOID

"For we dare not make ourselves of the number, or compare ourselves with some that commend themselves: but they measuring themselves by themselves, and comparing themselves among themselves, are not wise." 2 Corinthians 10:12 KJV

A lot of successful people get to be successful because they like to consider themselves driven. "I'm driven to succeed, I'm driven to change this organization, and I'm driven to help change other people's lives." In so doing, we often forget that a consistent passion for giving, leading, and success requires that we do a lot of self-care. What I run into a lot is self-care coupled with self-compassion issues. We are hard on ourselves, or we are busy trying to be like other people who look like they've got the keys to the kingdom. There's a little book out by Sandra Stanley called *The Comparison Trap*. She explores all of the ways women, especially, get caught up in comparing themselves with others, and the real biggie is not knowing how to handle the emotions that come with that.

This is apparently a part of the human condition because the scriptural choice for this chapter is at least a couple thousand years old. This is also learned behavior. Until around the third grade, my niece was totally expressive and very much her own person. Then something happened. Competition amongst her peers set in with a raw vengeance. Nothing was sacred! The pressure was on to dress, talk, write (or not), read (or not), participate in sports (or not), all on the basis of what her peers were doing.

Some of the girls rebelled by being extreme outliers at both ends of the curve, either being fully controlled or being completely different in any and every possible way. Those who managed to stay in the zone of loving themselves and not requiring an inordinate amount of outside approval had parents who taught them about self-love, being loved by God, being special in their own unique ways, and shared ways of being kind to themselves, even when others were not. The older, less self-compassionate and more group-compliant we become, the harder the negative self-talk is to stop. We become "driven" and measure our success by all the ways we persist in things that were never our own ideas in the first place. We also learn to mimic other people's emotional responses as our own.

I worked as COO to one of the finest, most giving, and driven CEO's in my community. To this day, he is a community treasure. However, this man was up at 4:00 am in the morning running five miles, and no matter how I tried, I could never get to work before he did, nor could I work later than he did. He would start meetings with physicians as early as 6:30 am and meet with them into the wee hours of the morning if necessary. And did I mention that I am not a morning person?

One day, as I was going nuts with the fatigue of trying to keep up with him, we had a talk about it. He asked me where I got the idea that he cared whether or not I could match hours with him. He told me that it was our differences in style and approach that created the success in our partnership as leaders. We became an incomparable and inseparable team with unmatched success in transforming our organization and the lives of the people we employed and those we served. I had the pleasure of succeeding him as CEO and President of that same organization.

Never since have I used another person as a yardstick for my performance. I make a point of being clear on my own strengths, maximizing them and allowing others to use their strengths to complement my weaknesses, while giving them credit where credit is due. And believe me, my closest friends are some bad chicks. I could lose my mind trying to compete with them!

Right away, when I'm in probably the very first session with my clients, I pay very close attention to the ways they express emotion. I look for clues of emotional incompetence. I look for negative emotions, like anger, resentment, sadness, and so many others. Rarely are successful people externally challenged by those around them on their expression of negative emotions. When someone is talking to me, I might say, "Wow, I notice that you seem sad or angry when you talk about that. Where do you feel that sadness or anger?"

Many clients will inevitably say, "What do you mean where do I feel it?" The reason they can't answer that question is because they've shut their emotions down so much that they don't even pay attention to what, where, or how they are feeling it in their bodies. They just get trapped in the influence of the feeling. Of course, the next thing that comes from suppressed negativity may be resentment. Someone will say, "I'm pissed off, but I don't know why."

One of the key questions I ask when I'm deciding if I'm going to take a client on is, "Have you ever done life coaching before?" Sometimes, if a person hasn't done this before, they might come in with the idea that my job is to tell them what to do. The "tell" is when someone says, "Well, I just don't know what my life purpose is. Are you going to tell me what it is?" My answer is, "No, I cannot."

"What would you really like life to be like? If money was no object, if relationship, creative expression, if none of these things were an object, what would you really want your life to look like?"

Sometimes another misconception is that I will magically get you unstuck. This is not magic; it's work. It's not hard work, though. It's just that it's work that requires absolute surrender. This is the type of surrender that successful people aren't particularly good at. It might feel at first like capitulating or losing. However, with coaching you must come in with the idea of surrendering to the fact that "I really don't know how to get unstuck, and I'm okay with that. I don't know, so whatever you can share that's useful, or however you try to show me how to do my life differently, I'm all in for that."

Of course, I'm not a dictator. This is not a dictator relationship. It's a partnership because I become your Partner in Believing. I'm going to partner with you and hold for you the idea that you are powerful beyond your imagination; and I will hold that for you when you can't hold it for yourself. This is not hard work, just disciplined work in a field of endeavor that might make you stretch emotional, mental, and spiritual muscles in a new direction. When I start with a client, I want to start with the end picture in mind so you can discipline yourself to get to the end picture. So I ask, "What would you really like your life to be like? If money was no object, if relationship, creative expression, if none of these things were an object, what would you really want your life to look like?"

FOOD FOR THE *JOURNEY*

Ask yourself, "What would I really like my life to be like? If money was no object, if relationship, creative expression, if none of these things were an object, what would I really want my life to look like?"

WHAT ABOUT MY RELATIONSHIPS?

"Love is patient, love is kind. It does not envy, it does not boast, it is not proud. It is not rude, it is not self-seeking, it is not easily angered, it keeps no record of wrongs. Love does not delight in evil but rejoices with the truth. It always protects, always trusts, always hopes, always perseveres. Love never fails."
1 Corinthians 13:4–8 NIV

"Every man in his lifetime needs to thank his faults."
- Ralph Waldo Emerson

It is not possible to have a coaching relationship without having to handle issues of the heart. In fact, my own success with clients depends on my ability to accept and see their goodness and strength no matter what I hear or see. Carl Rogers, the pioneer in humanistic psychology, calls this Unconditional Positive Regard (UPR). I just call it love.

Let's say I have a client who is successful, has been successful for a long time, but begins to notice their relationships, particularly the relationship with their significant other, is becoming less and less rewarding for either or both of them. Even though they know that they still absolutely love and adore the other, things have begun to be uncomfortable for them. Then they may begin to think, "You know, this job isn't really giving me the satisfaction it used to give me and that is spilling over into my love life." At that point, a wise person is either going to share with somebody who can help them or who will refer them to me, or grace will put us together. In desperation to get rid of the pain and to preserve valued relationships, Coaching becomes a great solution and gift to all the relationships in their lives, both present and future.

Life is like a beautiful tapestry. The picture on the top side is colorful, smooth, and perfect. The underside is just a mess, a tangled jumble of color until it is trimmed and bearing a vague resemblance to the topside. To get the beauty on the top requires the seeming confusion, crossed relationships, color mixing, knots, and clippings on the back. Following the pattern doesn't always seem to be working and sometimes we want to change the colors or the quality of the thread. And in life we get to do that.

Very often, clients refer spouses. Sometimes, it is because the spouse is so amazed at the transformation of the client that they want to try this for themselves. I have had wives call and sign up for a *Journey* out of gratitude for the restoration of the person they originally fell in love with! After one such event, I received a call from the husband who was the first of the couple to see me, followed by his wife. He happily announced that they were both courageously quitting their jobs and moving on to pursue their true passions.

On the other hand, some clients see me to resolve the resentment and anguish they feel when a spouse is sick or dying. There may be unfinished emotional business they need the courage to handle before the spouse dies. I have seen women with breast cancer and men with prostate cancer who take the *Journey* to resolve the emotional trauma, fear, and uncertainty that touches their work and their most important support relationships.

Life is like a beautiful tapestry. The picture on the top side is colorful, smooth, and perfect. The underside is just a mess, a tangled jumble of color until it is trimmed and bearing a vague resemblance to the topside. To get the beauty on the top requires the seeming confusion, crossed relationships, color mixing, knots, and clippings on the back. Following the pattern doesn't always seem to be working and sometimes we want to change the colors or the quality of the thread. And in life we get to do that. We even get to take breaks in the work. Yet, we still have to complete the picture and it cannot be done without all those threads touching, intersecting, breaking off, and changing some of the colors and quality of the thread.

Coaching is just another part of creating the picture of the life you would love to live. It can always enrich, enhance, and enable your relationships. There is virtually no way relationships are not touched in the process. I urge my clients to share the happenings and tools being learned on the *Journey* to the extent they are comfortable. Most often, though, clients are happier sharing their achievements, changes, and insights with their significant other, rather than the tool itself, unless tool-sharing is essential to the learning. It is also important that the client is given the option to disclose the *Journey* within relationship. Sometimes, a person is simply uncomfortable immediately disclosing the work they are doing.

When clients get to the crossroads about personal and professional relationships, someone has to ask the intrusive questions. "What does all this mean for you? What do you think this is about? What if you didn't have this job? What if you walked away? What if you found that you still love this person deeply, it's just that now's the time to move to a different way of experiencing each other? Are you willing to do that? Can you be that vulnerable? Are you okay taking 100% responsibility for how you adjust the relationship?" When the right questions are asked at the right time and the focus is on the client, amazing things can begin to happen.

A key step, of course, is to begin to focus on gratitude. I'm also a Christian Science Practitioner. I am no longer a member of the Christian Science Church, but I continue to value my training. When I was in training, the person who trained me shared the story of how when she first became a Christian Scientist, she went to a Practitioner and said, "I want to leave my husband." She had four children, was a great mom, and had really good reasons to want to end the marriage.

In the midst of the session, she realized that what she wanted was the Practitioner to give her permission to leave her husband, and the Practitioner wouldn't do it. What the Practitioner said to her was, "Well, is it harmonious?" When she just kept saying to her, "I just feel like I need to get a divorce," the Practitioner kept on asking, "Well, is it harmonious?" She said she thought in her mind, "What on earth is she talking about? I wouldn't want a divorce if it was harmonious." At the end of the session, the Practitioner asked her to come back to see her when "it was harmonious."

Spending time in gratitude begins to calm us down. We are then able to let go of blame, guilt, shame, and all those things that come when a successful person is suddenly finding themselves unsuccessful at something. It's just not okay to sweep our discomfort under the rug.

The thing I teach my clients is that no matter where you find yourself, you have to make it okay to be where you are. You've got to find a way to express and genuinely feel gratitude for what that experience is bringing to you. No blame, no shame, no demonizing the other, even if it's bringing to you a discomfort so profound that you want to flee!

We have to be able to give thanks for the experience. "I'm so thankful that what's going on with my boss is showing me those things inside of me that I don't want to do or be anymore." Or, "I am so grateful to my husband for all that I am learning in this relationship." Working through gratitude is always an intentional and important step with my clients. I firmly believe that you can't get something else until you are okay with and grateful for what you already have. Just learn to appreciate it for all that it brings you; the good, the bad, the sweet, the bitter. Then, and only then, is it *harmonious* and okay to make a decision to step away from it. Spending time in gratitude begins to calm us down. We are then able to let go of blame, guilt, shame, and all those things that come when a successful person is suddenly finding themselves unsuccessful at something. It's just not okay to sweep our discomfort under the rug.

We can all get to a place where leaving a situation is easier than bearing the pain. Now, this harmony-seeking is not the thing to do when you are in physical danger! But even if you flee for physical safety, at some point you will be faced with the need to make it harmonious in your own spirit!

Coaching is an organic process. While I have this great toolkit that I can draw from to help my clients, I don't know where it's going. I just know that it's a *Journey* and we're going to get off at some point, part ways, and we will each be better for having matriculated at EU together. I listen for where I need to go with my clients. Yeah, I have steps laid out for the *Journey* and all of that, but it is very, very organic. It is very client-tailored and focused. The roadmap depends entirely on my capacity to care, listen, speak, or not speak.

When I'm listening to my clients, I'm not just listening to the words coming out of their mouths; I'm listening for what the Holy Spirit is saying. I leave myself open to being a channel for their needs, a channel for hearing and addressing their needs, because I don't always know the answers either. I am always amazed by what comes to me in the midst of a session, and I go, "Oh, I thought we were going to do something else today, but this is what spirit wants us to do today." I think a good Coach has to be open to that. I don't think you're coaching fairly if you want to stick to your own agenda. After all, I represent a privileged, respectful, and important relationship in my client's life!

FOOD FOR THE *JOURNEY*

1. When you name it, you claim it. What will you name today? What will you name the rest of your life?
2. Can you express gratitude for every relationship in your life and what you are learning in it?
3. How is the tapestry of your life going? Do you want a new pattern, new colors, new thread, or better fabric?

WHO IS LUCY SHAW?

Lucy Shaw is a Senior-Level Executive with a Masters Degree in Business Administration and has practiced as a Naturopath, Registered Nurse, and Certified Nutritional Counselor. She is also a much sought-after Personal and Professional Life Coach, speaker, teacher, author, and motivator. Ambitious and excelling in everything she has done, Lucy rose through the ranks from bedside nursing in one of the largest and most prestigious private hospitals in the world to the position of President and Chief Executive Officer at the Regional Medical Center of Memphis, a safety net hospital.

At the time of her leadership, The Med was a 465-bed tertiary teaching hospital with 2,600 employees and a $300 million budget. Lucy is described as being "qualified to lead, motivate, and inspire by virtue of a strong record of success for her and those whose lives she has touched."

Lucy is well known for her expertise in financing and managing the care of the underserved. Her skills and abilities in those areas brought her before the United States Senate Finance Committee on several occasions and before colleagues as far away as Vienna, Austria. Her face has graced the cover of several magazines. She has served as Honorary Consul to New Zealand, on University and Bank Boards of Directors, and has published books and articles on health and management issues, as well as personal, spiritual, and professional development.

After completing major capital improvement projects, establishing the hospital as a leader in quality improvement, co-founding the first local university and medical center combined HMO, and preparing the medical center for a successful segue into the era of managed care, Lucy left the position of President and CEO of The Med in 1994 to start her own consulting business. As a Consultant and entrepreneur, she has applied her wide range of experience and skills in a diverse field of business applications and opportunities.

She currently serves in an active role as Chairwoman of the Board of Tri-State Bank of Memphis; is a national consultant, author, and speaker on Poverty for aha!Process, Inc.; and is a trainer for Transition to Success, which is a model for treating the condition of poverty. She is President/CEO of Life Works with Lucy Shaw.

Lucy has Coaching clients across the country and is a busy motivational speaker and teacher. She is a co-author of the book *Bridges to*

Health and Healthcare and author of *Be Not Anxious* and *Making Bricks without Straw*. Recently she began a project of institutionalizing Life Coaching for public education leadership and faculties. She has also developed and facilitates a Life Skills curriculum for returning citizens outside prison walls.

Lucy is happy to report that because she is a confident believer in the power of the Law of Circulation, she tithes of her time, talent, and treasure with intentionality to her church, where she is the Minister of Christian Leadership and Development.

Contact Lucy

www.lifeworkswithlucy.com

Telephone 901.483.7754

E-mail: lifeworkswithlucyshaw@gmail.com